The Outdoor Youth Adventures
Young Hunter's Coloring Book

W9-ARS-238

Top Brass Publishing
P.O. Box 209
Starkville, MS 39760

662-323-1559
Fax: 662-323-7466

Illustrated by Chuck Galey
Concept by Steve Madar, Arthur Cosby III and Eric Cosby

Printed in the U.S.A. All Rights Reserved.

Copyright ©2003

www.outdooryouthadventures.com

Code JEBFBJAJ

2

3

4

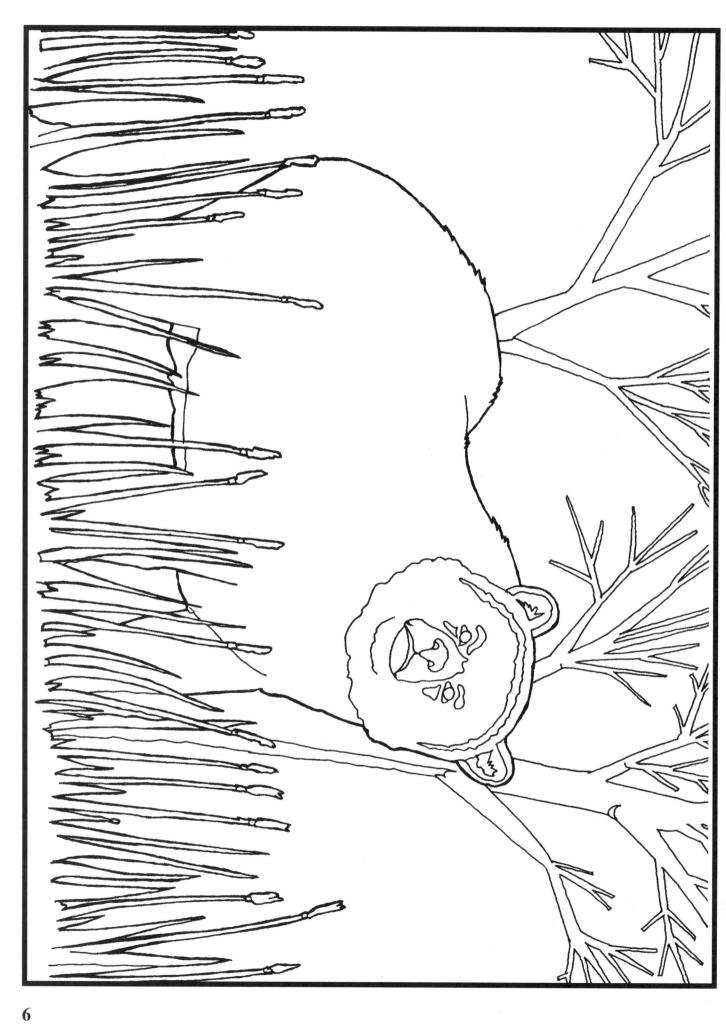

6

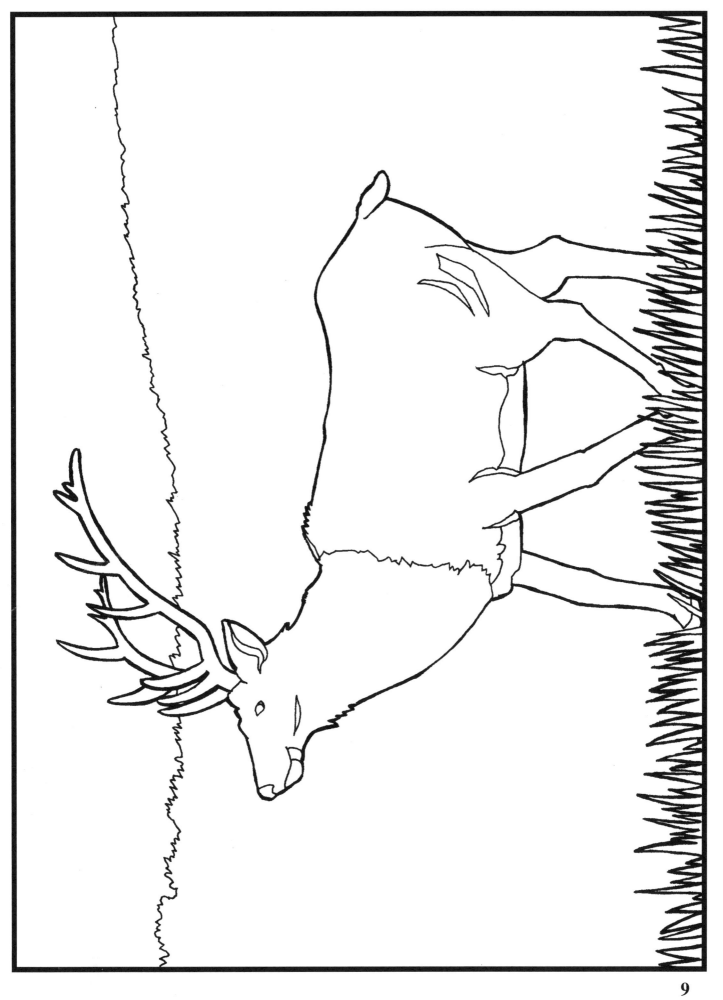

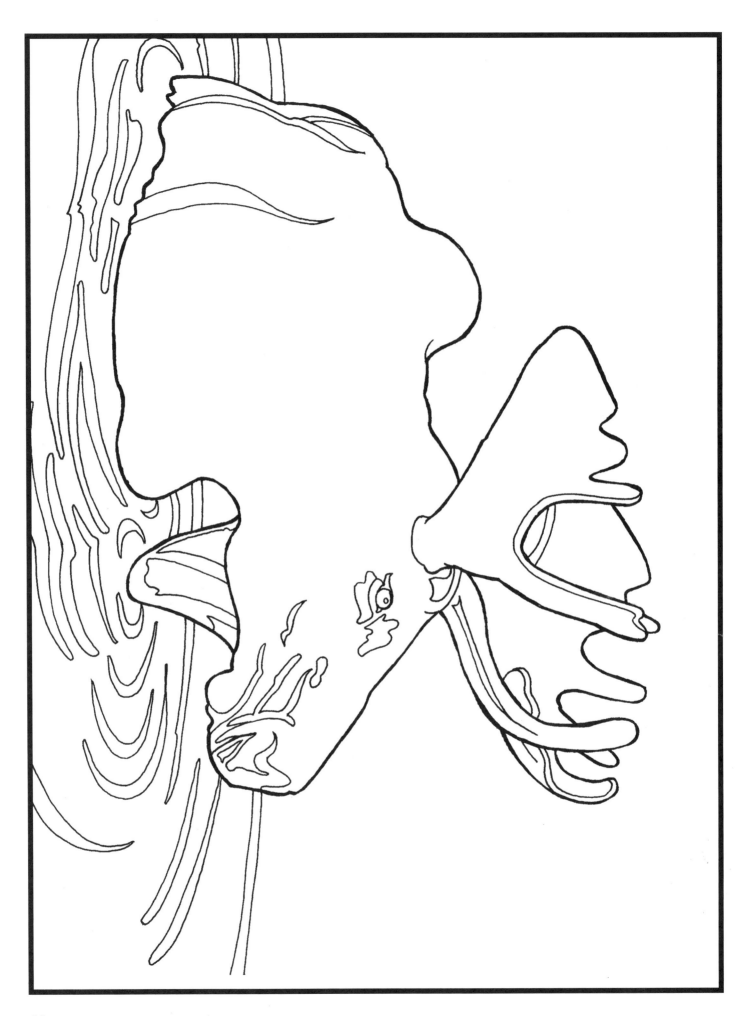

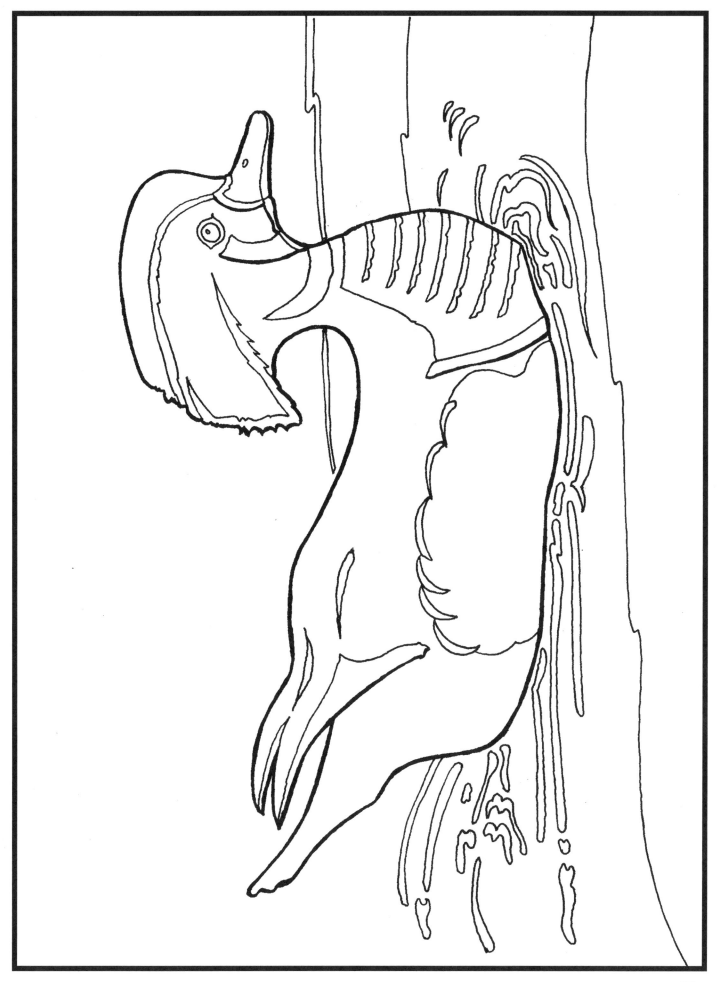

13

15

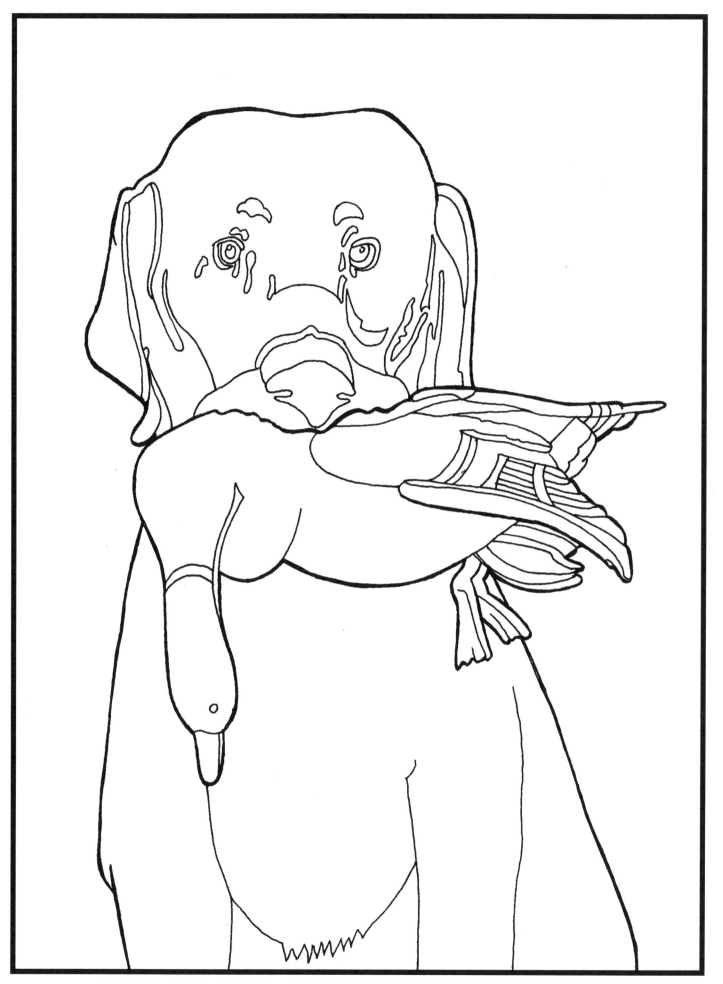

17

18

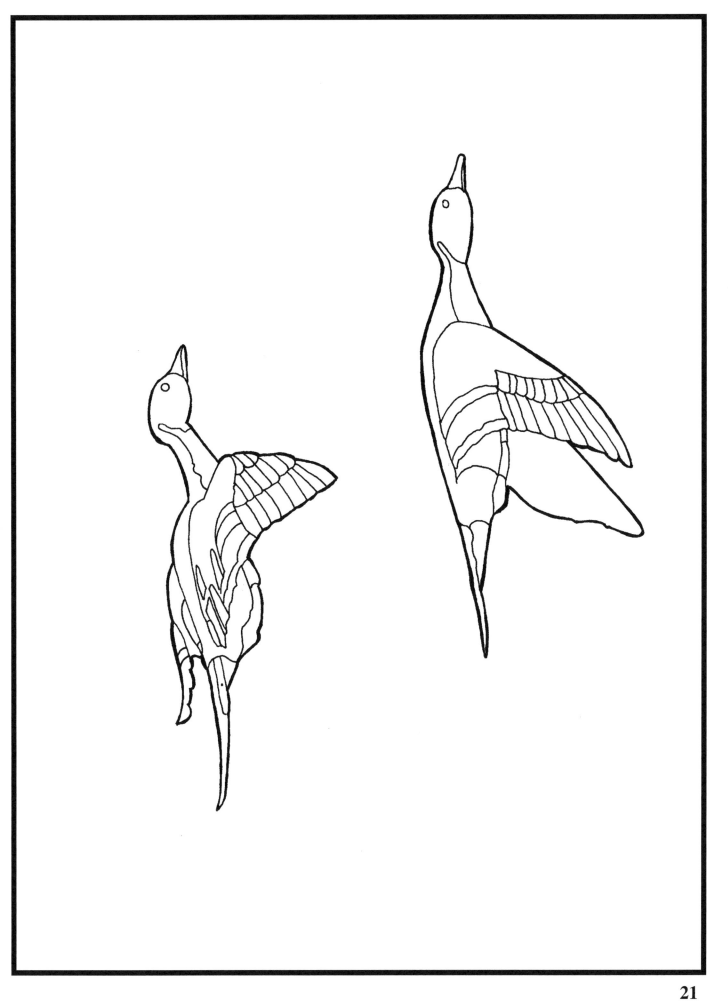

28

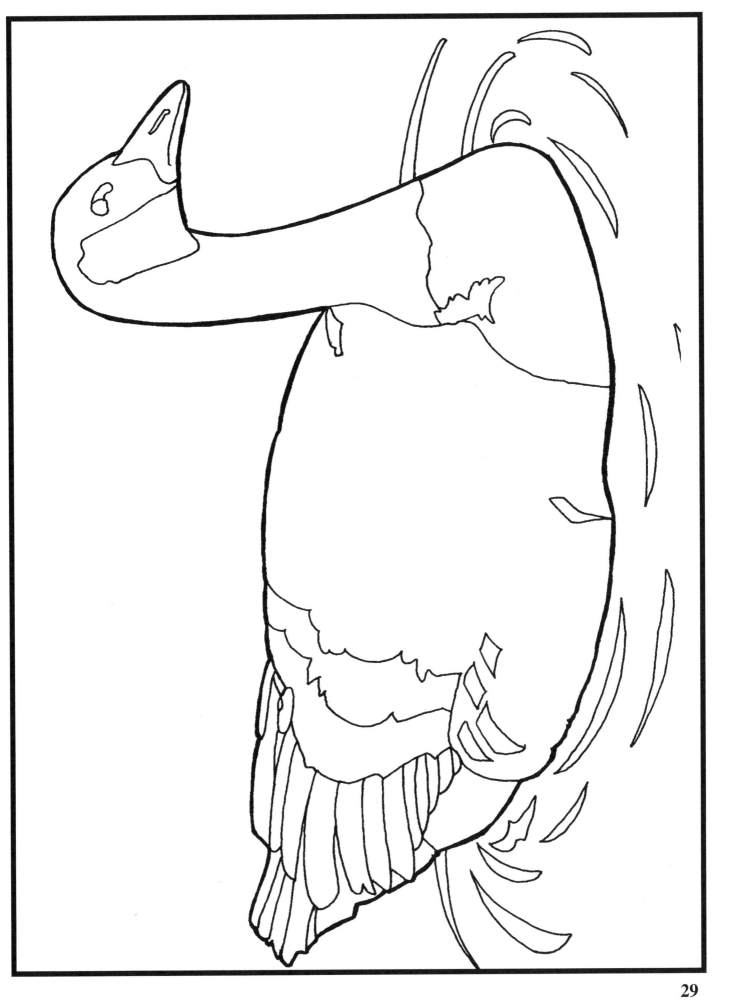

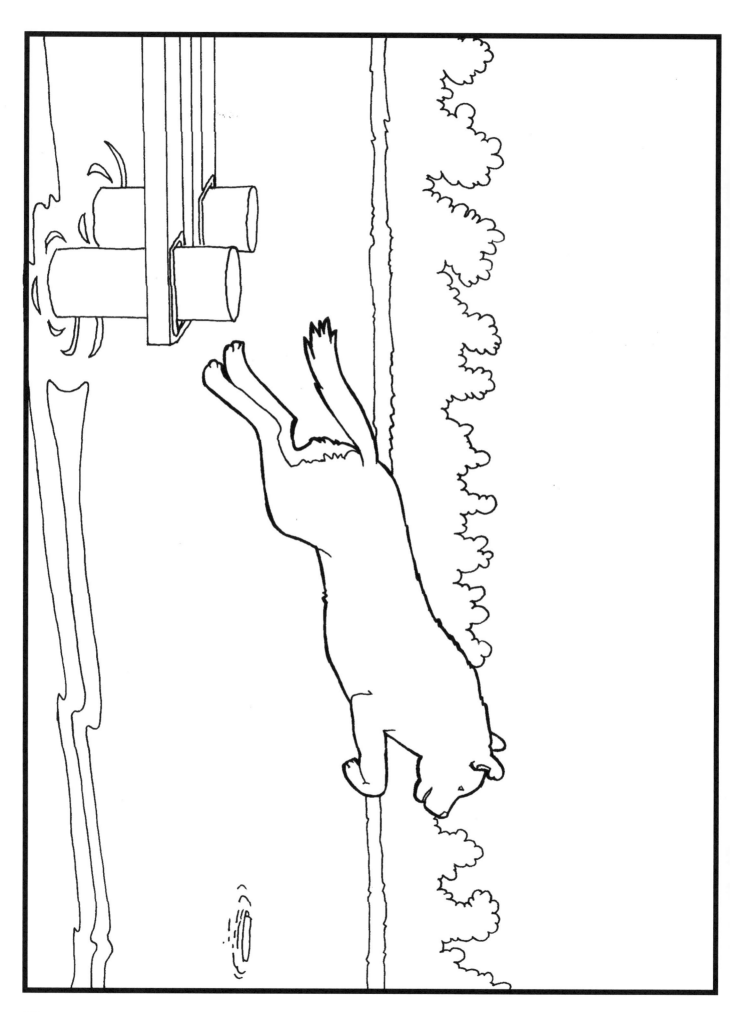

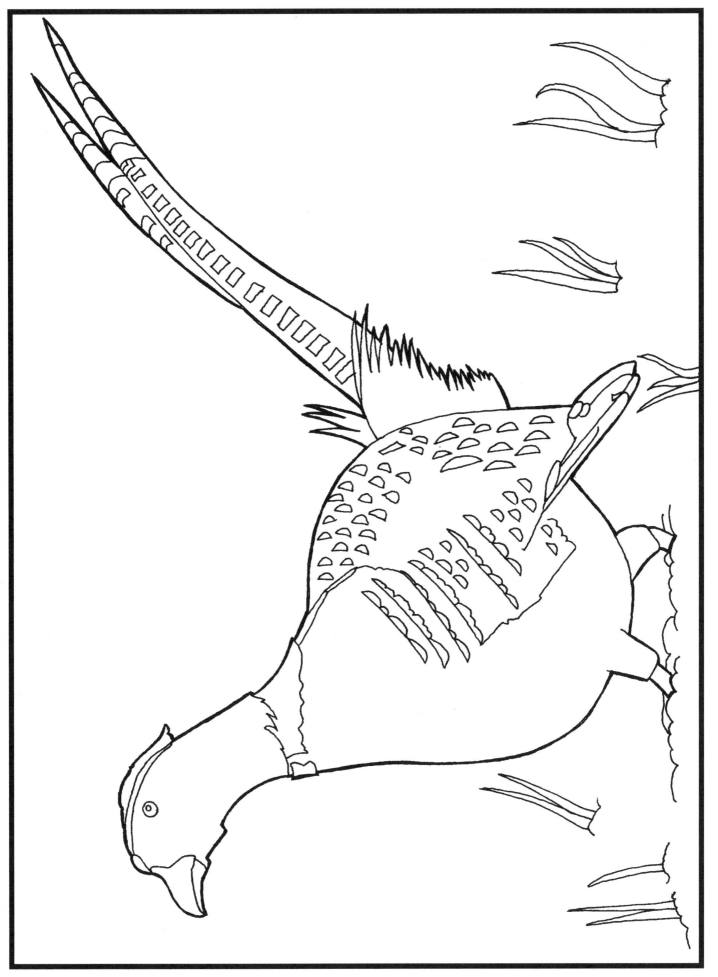

33

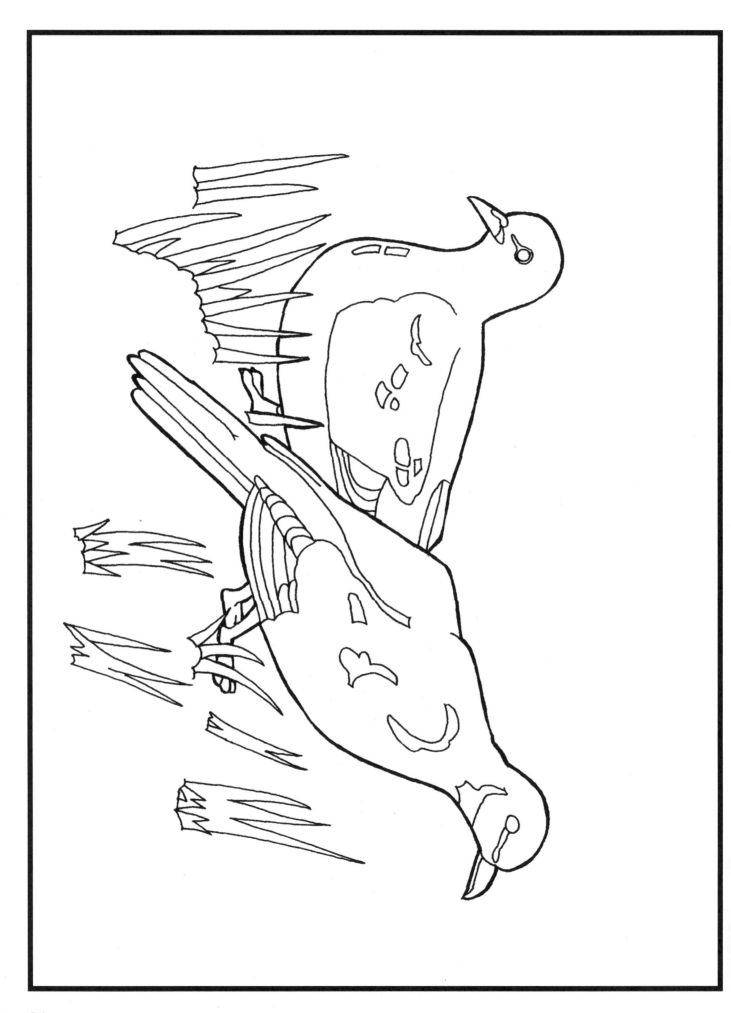

35

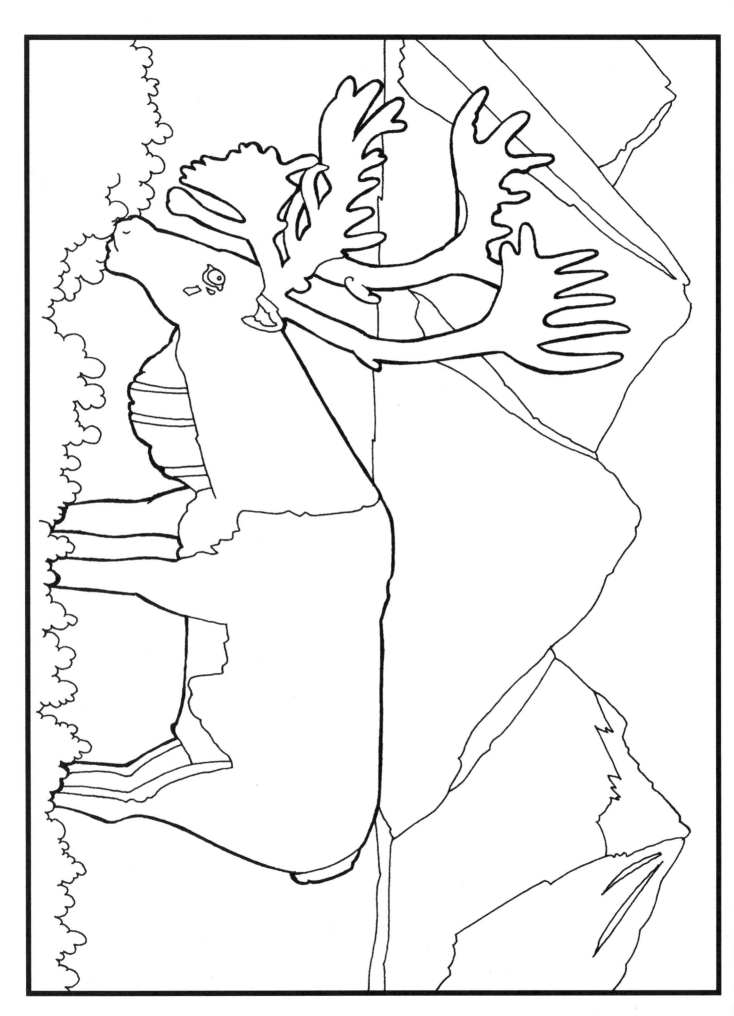

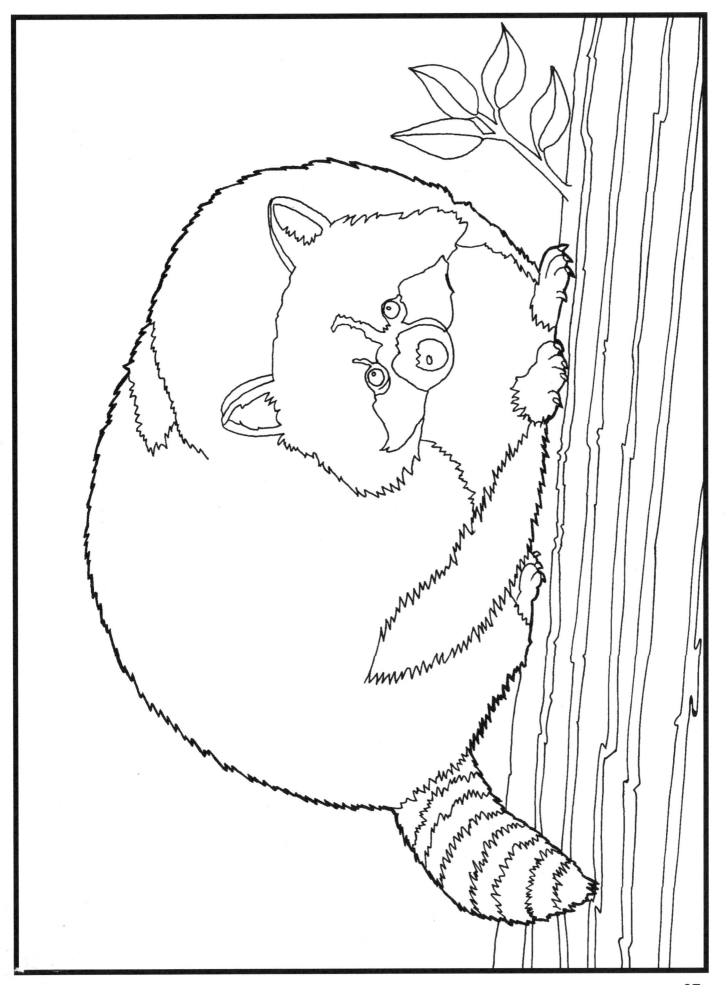

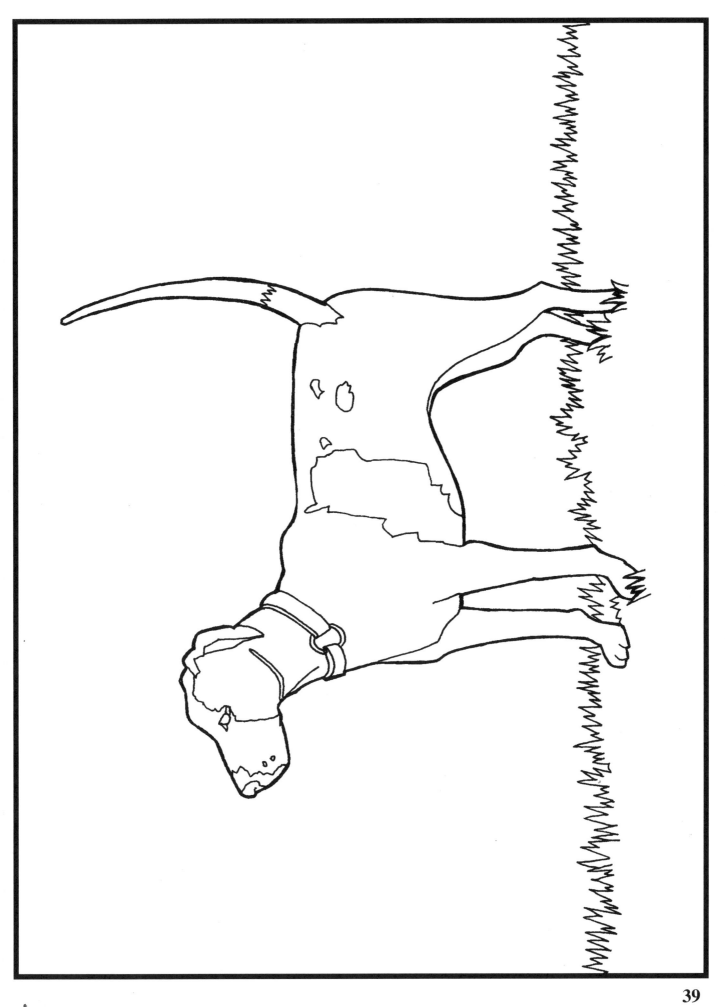

39

40

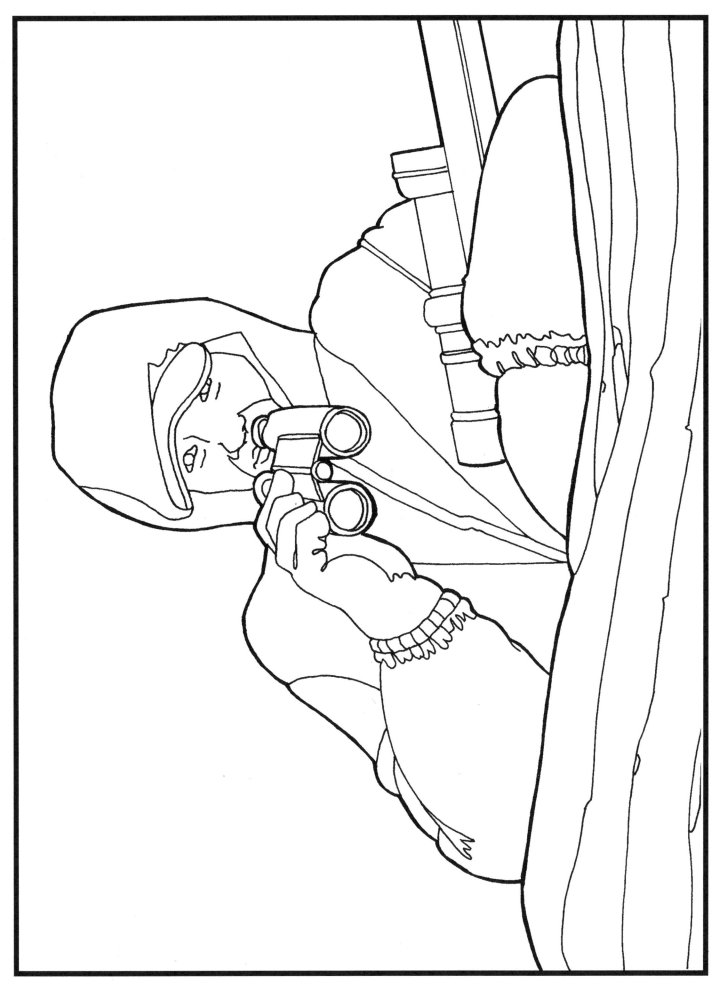

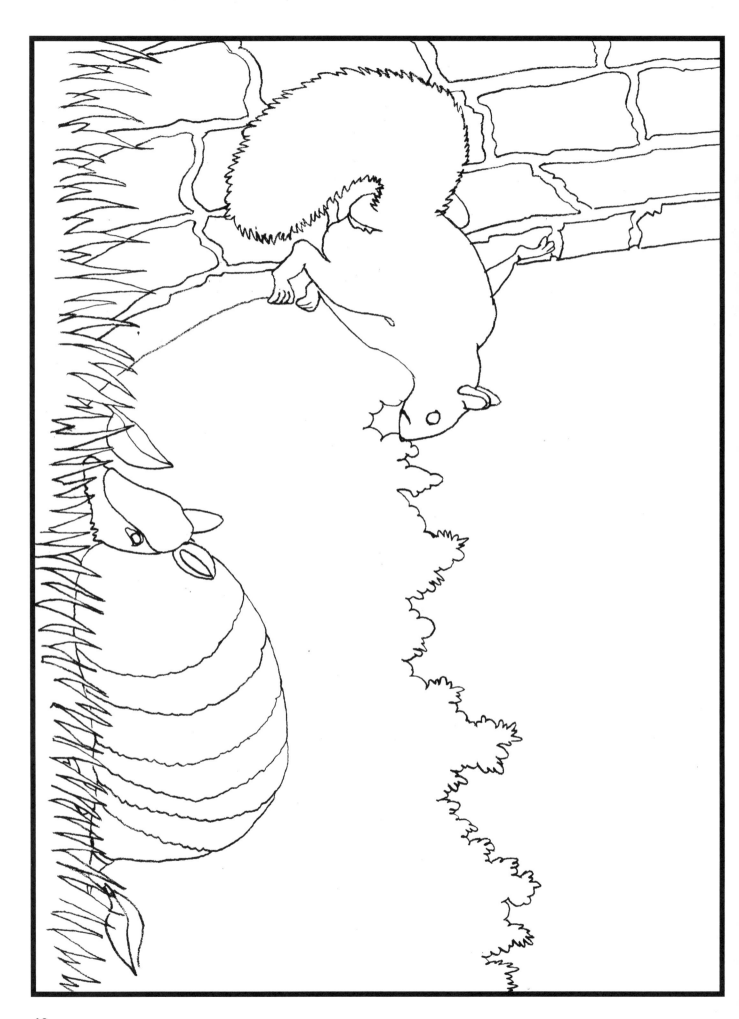

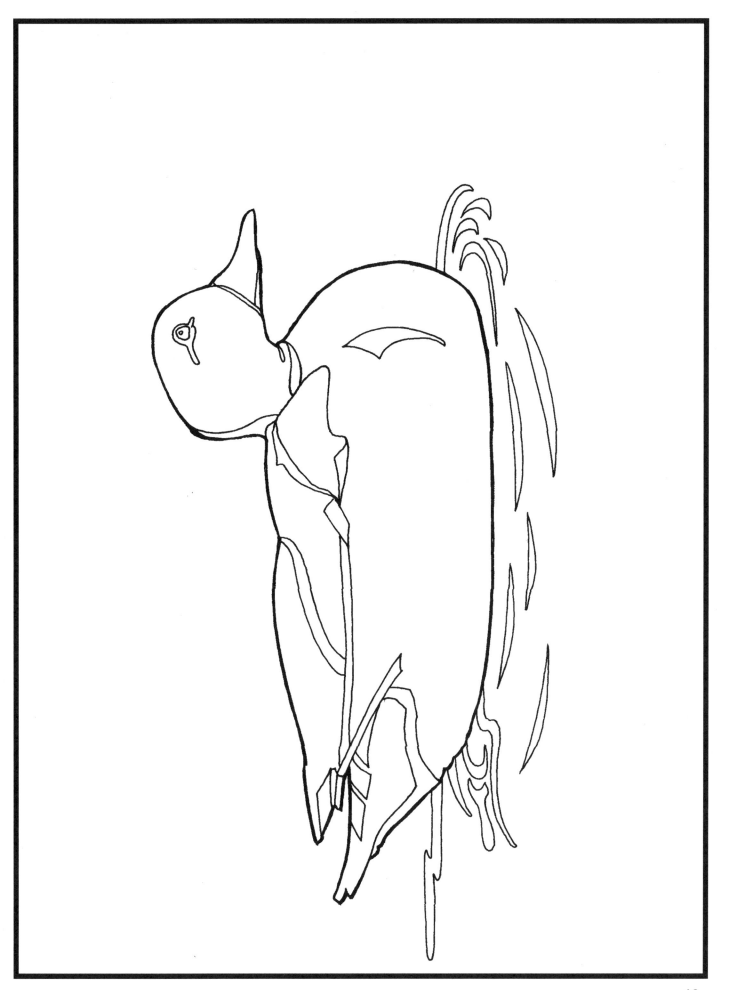

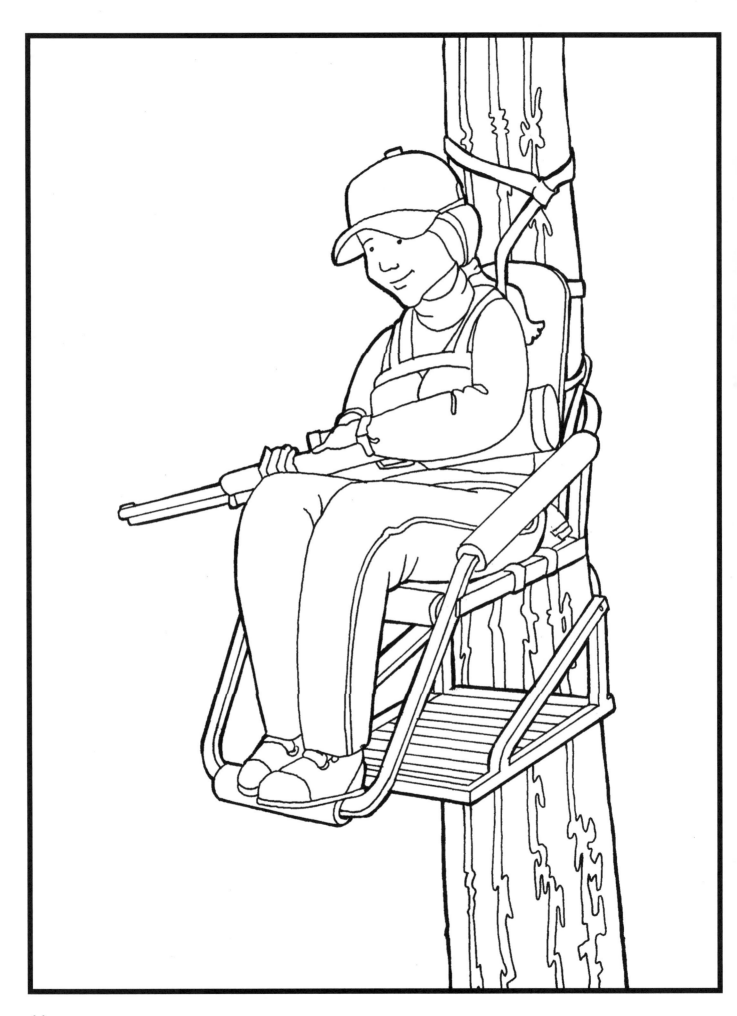

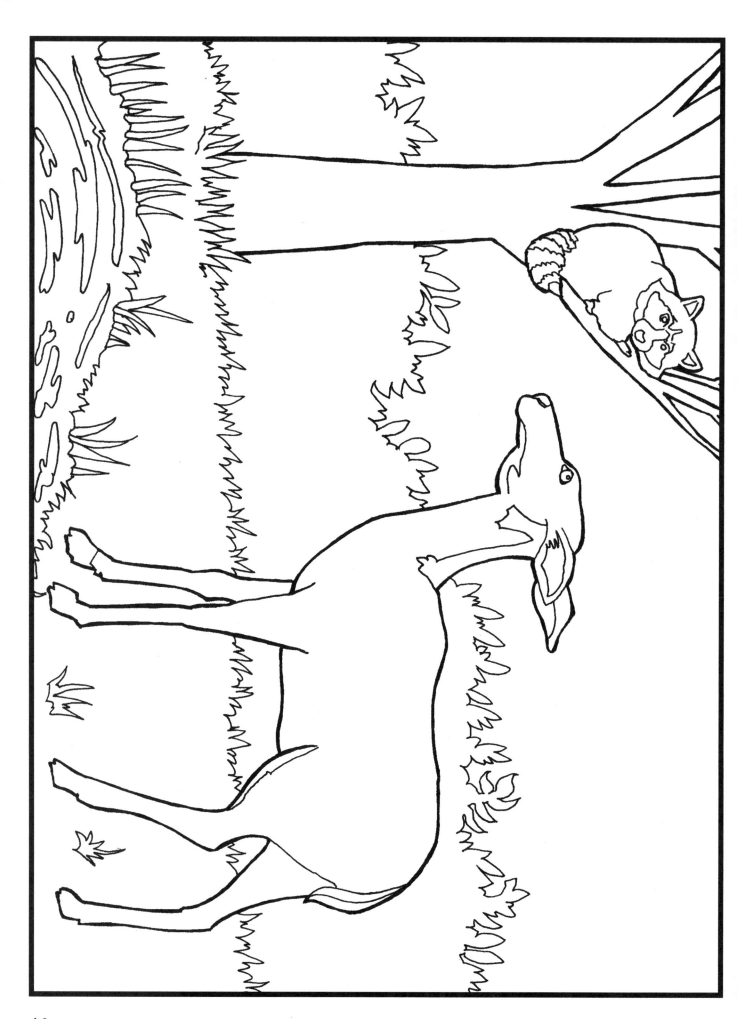

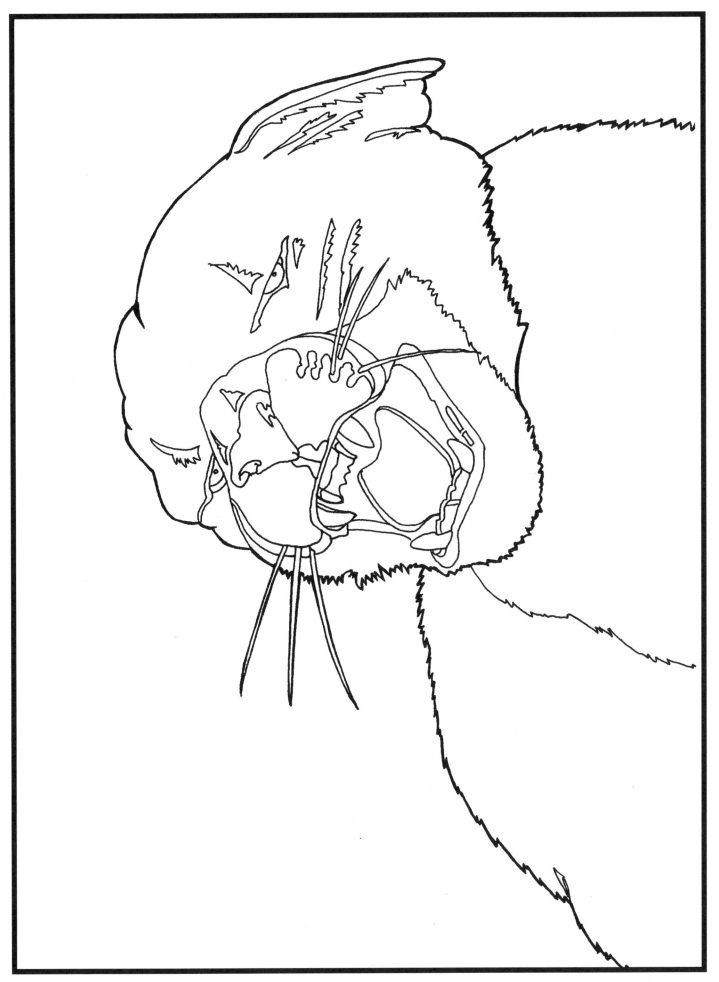